SUMMARY

OF

THE COMPLETE GUIDE TO FASTING

BY DR. JASON FUNG

Heal Your Body Through Intermittent, Alternate-Day, and Extended Fasting

BY

Dependable Publishing

COPYRIGHT

This publication is protected under the US Copyright Act of 1976 and other applicable international, federal, state, and local laws. All rights are reserved, including resale rights. You are not allowed to reproduce, transmit or sell this book in parts or in full without the written permission of the publisher. Printed in the USA. Copyright © 2019, Dependable Publishing.

DISCLAIMER

This book is a summary. It is meant to be a companion, not a replacement, to the main book. Please note that this summary is not authorized, licensed, approved, or endorsed by the author or publisher of the main book. The author of this summary is wholly responsible for the content of this summary and is not associated with the original author or publisher of the main book in any way. If you are looking to purchase a copy of the main book, please visit Amazon's website and search for **"The Complete Guide to Fasting: Heal Your Body Through Intermittent, Alternate-Day, and Extended Fasting *by Dr. Jason Fung"*.**

TABLE OF CONTENTS

INTRODUCTION 7
    KEY TAKEAWAYS 7
    SUMMARY 7

PART I: WHAT IS FASTING AND WHY IS IT GOOD FOR YOU? - CHAPTER ONE: WHAT IS FASTING? 11
    KEY TAKEAWAYS 11
    SUMMARY 11

CHAPTER TWO: A BRIEF HISTORY OF FASTING 18
    KEY TAKEAWAYS 18
    SUMMARY 18

CHAPTER THREE: BUSTING THE MYTHS OF FASTING 23
    KEY TAKEAWAYS 23
    SUMMARY 23

CHAPTER 4: THE ADVANTAGES OF FASTING 28

KEY TAKEAWAYS 28

SUMMARY 28

CHAPTER 5: FASTING FOR WEIGHT LOSS .. 31

KEY TAKEAWAYS 31

SUMMARY 31

CHAPTER 6: FASTING FOR TYPE 2 DIABETES 35

KEY TAKEAWAYS 35

SUMMARY 35

CHAPTER 7: FASTING FOR A YOUNGER, SMARTER YOU 38

KEY TAKEAWAYS 38

SUMMARY 38

CHAPTER 8: FASTING FOR HEART HEALTH 41

KEY TAKEAWAYS 41

SUMMARY 41

CHAPTER 9: WHAT YOU NEED TO KNOW ABOUT HUNGER 44

KEY TAKEAWAYS 44

SUMMARY 44

CHAPTER 10: WHO SHOULD NOT FAST? ... 47

KEY TAKEAWAYS 47

SUMMARY 47

PART II: HOW TO FAST: CHAPTER 11: KINDS OF FASTS AND BEST PRACTICES 50

KEY TAKEAWAYS 50

SUMMARY 50

CHAPTER 12: INTERMITTENT FASTING 53

KEY TAKEAWAYS 53

SUMMARY 53

CHAPTER 13: LONGER PERIODS OF FASTING 56

KEY TAKEAWAYS 56

SUMMARY 56

CHAPTER 14: EXTENDED FASTING 59

KEY TAKEAWAYS 59

SUMMARY 59

CHAPTER 15: FASTING TIPS AND FAQS 62

KEY TAKEAWAYS 62

SUMMARY 62

PART III: RESOURCES 65

RECIPES 67

NOTES 73

INTRODUCTION

KEY TAKEAWAYS

- Many kidney diseases are caused by type 2 diabetes.
- Low carb diet is better than the usual low-fat diet prescription.
- The "calories in, calories out" approach to explaining fatness is wrong.
- Insulin may reduce blood sugar, but it also causes weight gain.
- Insulin resistance causes type 2 diabetes.

SUMMARY

After my residency in internal medicine, I decided to take up study on kidney disease (nephrology, at the University of California, Los Angeles). A specific set of basic assumptions and descriptions are often attached to every area of internal medicine. In the case of nephrology, it is perceived as an area for good thinkers. Kidney disease is very intricate in nature, it involves a lot of electrolytes and fluids that have to be understood. I love this field of medicine. And by the year 2001, I came back to Toronto as a nephrologist.

Many kidney diseases result from type 2 diabetes. I have handled hundreds of such cases, and I observed that most people who had type 2 diabetes get obese. Given my interest in intricacies and my practice as a professional specializing in type 2 diabetes and obesity, I got interested in the intake of food, or simply diet and nutrition.

There wasn't much instruction on diets in the medical school, so my interest in diets was passive. However, by the middle of 2000s, I developed an uncommon interest in the field of nutrition and diet. As at that time, the low-carb diet evangelism (Atkins diet) was on the increase and everyone seemed to be trying it out with amazing results. As a medical doctor, I have been trained to believe that the arteries of people who go on low-carb diet will be endangered and so we recommend low fat diet instead. Not too long thereafter, several studies began to emerge, that show that low-carb eating is healthier than the conventional system we were advising patients to adopt.

Figuring Out What Causes Obesity
In my training as a physician, what I believed was that the only way to lose weight is to spend more calories than one consumes. This is what we term the "*CICO approach*" meaning "Calories in, calories out". But the Atkins diet strategy seemed to be disproving the entire CICO idea, people who used the format consumed calories and were losing weight as well.

It was difficult to accept initially, but the evidence was overwhelming. It all boiled down to a singular truth: the consumption of calories does not cause obesity. Obesity is a hormonal disorder (excessive secretion of insulin in the body leads to obesity). So, reducing the amount of insulin can thus bring about the loss of weight. To reduce insulin, one could fast from time to time or use the ketogenic diet plan.

Insulin and Type 2 Diabetes

In handling diabetic patients with type 2 diabetes, I discovered that treating type 2 diabetes did not tally with treating obesity. While insulin may be a right choice for obesity, most doctors like myself were administering insulin for both types of diabetes. Insulin reduces blood sugar, but it increases weight as well.

The two types of diabetes (1 and 2) are caused by high blood sugar levels, but what leads to the increase in sugar level, differs in the two types of diabetes. In type 1, the increase in the sugar level is as a result of insufficient insulin, therefore, making the taking of insulin the best solution in that situation.

Type 2 diabetes, on the other hand, is caused by the resistance of the body to insulin. In other words, there is more than enough insulin in the body, but the system no longer recognizes it and does not use it for its intended purpose. So, prescribing the intake of insulin in this case only translates to worsening the condition. Instead, you should be looking for a way to reduce insulin. The only solution seemingly was to make adjustments in patients' diets.

I tried helping my patients to inculcate new diet habits, so as to reduce insulin, but my efforts were all nipped in the bud. Most people were busy and did not just have the time to effect such changes. Apparently, it was difficult for people to stay off certain foods. But I began to realize that it can even be simpler to avoid food completely (that is, it may be easier to fast).

PART I: WHAT IS FASTING AND WHY IS IT GOOD FOR YOU? - CHAPTER ONE: WHAT IS FASTING?

KEY TAKEAWAYS

- Fasting is not starvation. Starvation is involuntary while fasting is deliberate.
- Fasting is therapeutic.
- There is no connection between good health and perpetual eating.
- Fasting facilitates weight loss.
- Fasting speeds up metabolism and increases the secretion of adrenaline.

SUMMARY

People often mistake fasting to mean starvation. But there are differences between fasting and starvation. When one is fasting, he is willingly not taking food. Sometimes it could be for spiritual reasons, At other times it could be for health reasons or for any reason one may find worthy. But with starvation, people suffer the "absence" of food. They are in lack and cannot provide food for themselves. The central difference lies in the fact that fasting is done voluntarily with a level of control. This is not the case with starvation.

There are already a number of teachings that stand against fasting. These are especially sponsored by the big food companies that seek to grow their market and advertise their products everywhere. And although fasting is therapeutic, its place seems to, gradually, being replaced by other practices that are not even conducive to health. People are always advised to eat their meals without skipping. This is even preached everywhere as though it is the priceless truth. The truth however, is that there is no significant connection between good health and perpetual eating. In fact, it is the opposite (fasting) that does the magic!

Fasting All-Stars Mark Sisson

Over time, I've read and known that fasting can help one age slower, I did not take it seriously and never tried to fast for that purpose. However, I was compelled to fast for 36 hours when I travelled overseas for an extended trip and there was no food available to eat. It was all surprising to find out that I did not reduce in mass after the fast, I rather felt stronger with a clearer head.

Many questions often arise when we speak about fasting, ranging from who can fast? How healthy is it? And will I lose weight? The answers remain that you can fast, it is very healthy and you will lose weight whenever you do not eat. Fasting is quite unpopular among people because it doesn't enrich food or drug manufacturers and they tend to hide it from people, lest they lose their customers.

But have ever considered why obesity and type 2 diabetes were not rampant in the 1970's as they are today? The answer is that at that time, people only ate three times a day. There were rarely occasions where people ate in-between meals. It was strictly breakfast in the morning, lunch at noon and dinner at night (but you should notice that this is equal to the 14-hour daily fast)!

But today, the case is almost completely different! Today, adults and children alike are encouraged to snack from time to time. As a result, people eat over six times daily! This is the reason for the current obesity epidemic in our society today.

What Happens When We Eat?

When we eat, the amount of food consumed is normally higher than what we really need to produce energy at the moment. A great percentage of the consumed food is therefore required to be stored for later use. The process of storing energy is majorly controlled by insulin which tends to increase during feeding.

Insulin serves two key purposes. It assists the body to start utilizing energy by facilitating the entrance of glucose directly into the cells of the body, which in turn use the glucose for energy. Secondly, insulin helps the body to store energy when in excess. Energy can be stored in two ways: either as a pile of glucose known as glycogen or as fat. The fat is usually formed when the body reaches its glycogen-storing limit. The glycogen is stored in the liver. The fat is also deposited in the liver and other fatty portions in the body. There is a limit to the amount of glycogen that the body can be store away, but there is no limit to the amount of fat that can be stored away.

What Happens When We Fast?

When we fast, the reverse of the feeding process occurs. There is a reduced level of insulin and the body is signaled to use stored up energy, especially the glycogen stored in the liver and the liver can store as much as can sustain energy requirements for a day. After the it must have exhausted the glycogen, the body goes ahead to use body fat stored away.

This is simply natural. Humans have lacked food in the past and our bodies have adapted to this trend by developing sustenance mechanisms. This also means that there are no health implications associated with this process, it only helps us to keep surviving instead. The case of improper feeding is not the same thing.

Insulin Goes Down

One of the most significant happenings that accompany fasting is the reduction in insulin. The intake of all food increases insulin, especially carbohydrates, so when we do not take food at all, insulin is reduced. This translates to favorable conditions in the body like the increased sensitivity to insulin. Usually, when there is excess insulin, the body tends to develop resistance (as in type 2 diabetes). But this time around, it is reduced and the body is forced to recognize it. When insulin is lowered, it also helps the body to eliminate excess water and salt.

Electrolytes Remain Stable

The body has established ways of maintaining electrolytic balance during fasting, so as to maintain health. Different studies have found that fasting never led to imbalances in the electrolytes, even when it is prolonged.

Adrenaline Increases and Metabolism Speeds Up

There is a general belief that fasting will leave one weak and unable to do certain things, but this is not so. Most people who had fasted testified that they felt renewed and energized during fasting. This is because the body still obtains fuel from stored energy and again, adrenaline promotes the release of stored energy.

Growth Hormone Goes Up

Together with adrenaline, cortisol and growth hormone assist in maintaining the availability of glucose in the body. They are counter-regulatory hormones because they work in antithesis with insulin, reducing its effect and bringing about increased blood sugar levels. Growth hormones may also stimulate enzymes like lipoprotein lipase and this translates into steady availability of fuel from fats. Meals suppress the production of growth hormones by far. The more you eat, the less growth hormones are secreted. Fasting on the other hand increases growth hormones significantly.

Benefits for Athletes

For athletes, they can maintain leanness within the fasting period. And the increased level of adrenaline during that period helps them to do more intense workouts, while increased growth hormones assist them to recover from the workout.

The Importance of Healthy Eating

Do not make the mistake of considering fasting to be the solution to all problems. There is yet need to feed properly. To feed healthily does not mean a combination of the three macro nutrients, carbohydrates, protein and fats, the focus should be on eating food, not specific foods. Overall, you need to:

- Eat unprocessed whole foods

- Reduce sugar and refined grains.

- Eat more natural fats

- Eat less artificial fats

- Balance feeding with fasting

Different Kinds of Fasting

Fasting maybe done in various ways as one may deem fit. It could an absolute fast where neither food nor water is taken. Many people undergo this type of fast for religious purposes. But medically, we usually do not encourage absolute fasting.

There are also various schedules for fasting. Fasting could be less than twenty-four hours (short fast) or longer than twenty-four hours (longer fasts). When fasting exceeds three days it becomes extended fasting.

CHAPTER TWO: A BRIEF HISTORY OF FASTING

KEY TAKEAWAYS

- Fasting was commonplace in the ancient era because food was relatively scarce.
- Fasting is an age-long practice, it did not begin today.
- Many religions practice fasting to draw closer to God and become free of sin.
- Fasting is a better way of treating sicknesses than drugs.
- Fasting can improve life expectancy.

SUMMARY

Today, it is common to find people who eat and take snacks at all times, but this was not the case many years ago. In fact, food was not as common as it is today, it was relatively scarce. Owing to wars, drought, insect infestations, diseases, and uneven seasons, food supply was irregular.

As the area of agriculture gained more attention and development, several food items can now be made available in-season and out-of-season. Large scale farming also saved the situation to a great extent.

However, inhabitants of these ancient times (like people of the Greek extraction), believed that there were underlying benefits associated with fasting. So even as food became more plentiful, they still fasted willingly. It was often described as cleansing or detoxification process, deeply honored and practiced to effect healing. This all shows that fasting is not new, it has been there in different societies and it has been practiced by various religious groups for eons.

Spiritual Fasting

One of the most significant commonalities shared by most religions is fasting. For example, the leading figures and initiators of Christianity, Buddhism, and Islam (Jesus Christ, Buddha, and Muhammad) alike believe fasting to be a powerful healing practice.

We can find an instance from the biblical story of Adam and Eve. They were forbidden from nothing but eating from a particular tree. But following the serpent's temptation, Eve betrayed God's trust, which implies that fasting is a means of staying away from temptation and staying within the place of God's trust and love.

Also, the Bible recounts of how Jesus spent forty days and forty nights in the wilderness fasting without any food (Matt. 4:2) The Bible states that he was hungry, was tempted by the devil but he overcame. Among Christians, fasting is a means of getting rid of fleshly influences and connecting to God in readiness for his manifestation.

Fasting All-Stars Abel James

Fasting as it were, was seen as a normal practice in the earlier generations. Now, so many spiritual implications are attached to it. Among Greek Orthodox Christians, one had to follow a fasting plan on 180 to 200 days of each year. This was done to improve life expectancy.

Among Buddhist monks, fasting was done to suppress the desires of the flesh so that it would become easier to attain *nirvana*. Hindus too are not left out. They believe that the more you fast, the more your sins are remitted for. It may also be done during festivals and specific days of the week/month are usually mapped out for fasting,

In Islamic religion, fasting is usually done during the holy month of Ramadan as prescribed by Prophet Muhammad in the Qur'an. It is obligatory for all Muslims and the fasting is without any water or liquid (absolute fasting).

The Early Adopters

Often called the father of modern medicine, Hippocrates was a harbinger of fasting, he was able to understand that obesity was an escapable disease. For Hippocrates, people who are lean are less likely to die suddenly. He prescribed one-time daily feeding for obese people together with regular exercising (notice that this equals the daily twenty-four-hour fast).

Another proponent of fasting was Plutarch, a writer/historian from Greece. He advised that instead of taking drugs, people should fast. Plato and Aristotle were also great heralds of the benefits of fasting. Generally, the ancient Greeks had this belief that fasting was a natural means of handling sicknesses. They also believed that mental health could be improved through fasting.

Other people like Paracelsus, Benjamin Franklin, Mark Twain also took positions in favor of fasting as a necessary practice, especially for health.

Modern Fasting

Around the middle of the 1800s and the beginning of 1900s, fasting was done for the sake of entertainment, people abstained from food for long periods of time just to entertain others. In those times anyway, hunger was rampant. Disease was common and wars overwhelmed the people, so obesity was not much an issue to tackle.

By 1915, it was then known (as seen in medical journals) that fasting was not harmful and could be the most viable option for people who suffer from obesity.

Fasting All-Stars Amy Berger

Although fasting had been an age-long practice, it has not been a regular and appreciated practice in the last three decades or more. People get cajoled for only mentioning it, not to talk of practicing it. However, if it is true that diseases like type 2 diabetes and obesity were caused by excess eating, then nothing can solve it as simply as eating less!

CHAPTER THREE: BUSTING THE MYTHS OF FASTING

KEY TAKEAWAYS

- Fasting does not decrease the metabolism rate of the body.
- When we fast, our body only changes its source of energy.
- The body monitors blood sugar level and this cannot be influenced by fasting.
- Fasting does not consume the muscles.
- Muscle can be gained through exercising, not diet.

SUMMARY

Regardless of the truth that fasting has been in practice over the past ages, yet there are still various myths that becloud our understanding of fasting and sometimes discourage people from fasting. These myths include the following:

Myth 1: Fasting Puts You in "Starvation Mode"

Starvation mode myth suggests that the metabolism rate of the body is reduced during fasting, and that the body becomes dysfunctional. This is quite absurd to believe. If one feeds three times daily for one year, there is no how a day without food would become problematic. We can justify this by considering the basic metabolic rate of our body. The basic metabolic rate is not fixed. It either decreases or increases in line with a lot of factors. If we burn many calories, we are likely to remain warm even in extremely cold weathers because the body generates its own heat within.

This also means that whenever the intake of calories reduces, the basic metabolic rate will also reduce while excess eating increases it. This is where the misconception lies; people consider the reduction in basic metabolic rate as a sign of a dysfunction in the body. The truth is that metabolism actually increases during fasts, because the body will have to use the energy stored away. There are hormones in the body which direct the body to utilize body fats when food is not available, these things do not reduce basic metabolism rate, they take it higher.

Fasting All-Stars Dr. Bert Herring

This myth is sustained by the consistent push of food marketers to make people consume the food they sell. The adverts usually come in forms that convince people that the absence of food could lead to unnecessary reduction in performance. The truth however remains that our bodies function effectively when we fast, it is only our source of energy that has changed.

Myth 2: Fasting Makes You Burn Muscle

There is yet another fallacious belief that surrounds fasting, people think that once we are not eating, our body utilizes the muscles to generate energy. This is not so. Energy is stored up as fat in the body and is utilized when food is not available. A study shows that fasting done alternately for about seventy days reduced the weight of the body by 6%. The fat mass reduced by 11.4% while the lean mass (bone and muscle) remained untouched. As a matter of truth, protein, like muscles, is spared during fasting. The switch is between the consumed food and the stored fat.

Fasting All-Stars Abel James

Muscle is gained or lost only by exercising not directly by eating. Fasting cannot consume the muscles because the body lacks food. Fasting consumes glycogen and fat, not muscles! The body takes recourse to these deposits to stay alive in the absence of food. If your concern is about gaining muscle, then take up an exercising program. Diet and exercise are not the same thing.

Myth 3: Fasting Causes Low Blood Sugar

The body has its way of monitoring blood sugar levels, fasting does not affect this. The myth that you will sweat and shake during fasting is very far from the truth. When you fast, the body breaks the glycogen in the liver to provide energy. This happens usually at nights to keep your blood sugar in check.

Myth 4: Fasting Results in Overeating

People also believe that just like we pay oxygen-depth after ceasing breath for a long time or doing tedious tasks, we will also be compelled to eat excessively to repay for the period of fasting. This is never the case. When fasting is done perpetually, appetite for food decreases instead and one is not likely to eat much. It causes people to lose weight and the same time maintains their new weight.

Myth 5: Fasting Deprives the Body of Nutrients

Apart from the case of children, breastfeeding mothers and pregnant women, fasting is a very wonderful option. When you fast, you do not change the food you eat, it is only the timing that changes, people get to their usual feeding plan after or before the fast. In this way, neither the micronutrients nor macronutrients will become deficient.

Myth 6: "It's Just Crazy"

When people are unable to find any other reason to dis-engage from fasting, they resort to describing it as "crazy". There is nothing crazy about fasting. Obesity is normally a product of overfeeding. And tackling obesity can also be based on reduced food intake. Fasting is important for losing weight. Isn't it mere common sense that staying without food will amount to loss of weight?

CHAPTER 4: THE ADVANTAGES OF FASTING

KEY TAKEAWAYS

- Fasting is a better option than following different dietary plans.
- It is very easy to fast.
- It costs nothing to fast. Actually, it costs less tan nothing to fast because you don't have to spend money on feeding yourself if you are fasting.
- Fasting can be scheduled and re-scheduled - it is flexible.
- Fasting is very powerful and effective for reducing insulin levels.

SUMMARY

Weight loss is one of the widely acclaimed benefits of fasting. But besides weight loss, there are many other benefits of fasting.

One may argue that having or following certain diet plans will have a great impact, but you can never compare dieting to fasting. This is because many factors make people to abandon their prescribed diet plans. Sometimes it could economic issues. At other times it could be tight schedules that disrupt people's ability to follow through on diet plans. I have discovered while treating many of my patients that diets do fail from time to time and because of this failure, it does not serve the purpose of treating sicknesses as much as fasting does.

Here are the various Advantages of fasting:

Advantage 1: It's Simple

Many times, my patients become confused on which kind of diet to consume, after all there is no generally accepted best diet type (low-calorie, low-fat, low-carbohydrate or low-sugar). Fasting resolves the entire confusion by just not eat anything (during controlled times).

Advantage 2: It's Free

Fasting is free of charge(s), and apart from being free, it also saves the cost of feeding. You do not need to purchase food items at all before you fast unlike the dietary approach.

Advantage 3: It's Convenient

The process of fasting saves one the most precious things in life – time. You do not need to spend time planning on what to cook, time spent on shopping, the cooking itself and the after-cooking cleaning, etc. This also solves the issue of eating outside the house. Fasting practically involves doing nothing, It cannot get any easier than that.

Advantage 4: You Can Enjoy Life's Little Pleasures

Fasting helps you to strike a balance in the things that you consume and do not consume. People have been advised to avoid certain foods which could increase weight, but if you fast from time to time, you may not always need to abstain from such things. Fasting occasionally will balance everything out.

Advantage 5: It's Powerful

Fasting is the quickest way to reduce insulin and of course insulin resistance. This also means that it is the most powerful way to tackle diseases like type 2 diabetes and obesity. No drug can be more efficient. All drugs are limited in dosage, above which they become harmful. And at that point, you would need to change drugs if you still have the disease.

Advantage 6: It's Flexible

Fasting can be done at any time and to any length. There are no specifications in time and duration, thereby making it dynamic. In other words, you do not need to follow a schedule, you draft your fast to suit you effectively.

Advantage 7: It works with Any Diet

Fasting does not choose the kind of food you eat. It can work with any kind of food. Weather you take grain or cheese or whatever, you can still fast.

CHAPTER 5: FASTING FOR WEIGHT LOSS

KEY TAKEAWAYS

- Dieting solves weight issues only on temporary basis.
- Low-calorie and low-fat diets do not solve the problem of being overweight.
- Insulin transports glucose from the bloodstream to the cells.
- Bariatric surgery can be used to remove stomach fats.
- Animal protein can increase insulin in the body.

SUMMARY

One thing about dieting for weight loss or for any other purpose is that it tends to produce only short-term results, after the initial cut-down in weight, people will still get back to their usual weight, if not higher this time.

"Eat Less, Move More" Doesn't Work

Over the past few decades, the general teaching has always been to go on low calories. Low-this or low-that dietary approach is seen as great for obesity. However, we can see from studies that this has only succeeded in increasing the rate of obesity. In 1995, reports said that no state in the U.S had obesity levels above 20%. But by 2015, the reverse became the case: no state has obesity levels below 20%.

It is not as if people no longer listen to the advice of doctors, after all, smoking had reduced because doctors warned against it. So, why is it difficult to get similar result with dietary practices? Reports show that the guidelines presented by the health industry are closely followed by the populace, but the expected result is never seen. This clearly shows that the "eat less, move more" advice is either not workable or completely wrong.

All studies have proven that despite the low-calorie, low-fat diet practice, people are not losing weight enough to record success. Those who lose a little tend to become fat again in a short while.

The solution to this is that we need to adopt a new advice, a new strategy and that new strategy is fasting.

Why "Eat Less, Move More" Fails: How Our Bodies Really Use Calories

This method fails because it is based on an untrue belief of how the human body utilizes calories (that is the single compartment model). This model presumes that the body breaks down every food into simple calories, stores the calories as a single compartment, and then utilizes the calories for exercise and metabolism. The model is a mere fabrication, it never existed.

There are instead two ways that calories are stored in the body, as glycogen or as body fat. When we feed, the body only stores excess glucose and fat, excess protein is converted to glucose and stored in the liver as glycogen. However, the liver cannot store every glucose, it has limited capacity. When the liver has reached its limit, the energy is then stored as fat in various areas of the body. This stored energy - fat and glucose can be used as source of energy during fasting but not in the same amounts or time. Glycogen is preferred by the body over fat, primarily because it is easier to digest.

Insulin plays a crucial role in the gain/loss of weight. Insulin level is usually low when we do not eat, and this helps the body to get to the fat deposits faster. The body cannot burn both glycogen and fat at the same time, but the low insulin levels gives the body quicker access to the fats, thereby reducing weight.

One of the primary functions of insulin is to transport glucose to the cells from the bloodstream, so that it can serve as energy. If, however, you have insulin resistance, your cells become insensitive to insulin, regular amounts of insulin will no longer be sufficient to facilitate the process. This often results in the accumulation of glucose in the body. The body in its balancing mechanism will secrete more insulin to force the process through, leading to high insulin levels in the body and invariably, it becomes difficult to burn the fat in the body.

The solution to high insulin levels and its attendant insulin resistance is fasting, though low-carb diets also reduce insulin levels, but you must also note that protein (especially animal protein) increases insulin as well. The best option is to fast. That way, insulin levels are reduced, the body accesses fat more easily and weight loss is assured.

Bariatric Surgery; an Argument for Fasting

Bariatric surgery is a surgical procedure undergone to reduce body/stomach fat. It is also capable of reversing type 2 diabetes. It works because it enforces reduction in calories. All of its results can also be produced through fasting without complications.

Bariatric surgery is associated with many after-surgery complications including scarring - narrowing of the esophagus, etc. Studies show that fasting is more effective in weight loss than bariatric surgery. So why would one subject one's self to surgery, when one could easily fast to produce the same or better results?

CHAPTER 6: FASTING FOR TYPE 2 DIABETES

KEY TAKEAWAYS

- Type 1 Diabetes results from insufficient insulin.

- Type 2 Diabetes is caused by excess insulin in the body.

- Insulin resistance means non-responsiveness of the body to insulin.

- Insulin was discovered in 1921.

- Type 1 Diabetes can be treated by injecting patients with insulin.

SUMMARY

There are basically two types of diabetes, type 1 and type 2 diabetes. These two forms of diabetes are seemingly on two opposite extremes. Type 1 is called an autoimmune disease where the body destroys certain insulin-generating organs, resulting in insufficient amount of insulin in the body. Type 2 on the other hand is caused by excess amount of insulin, which the body produces when it senses too much sugar in the blood. This often leads to insulin resistance - insensitiveness to insulin.

In type 1, insulin is lacking, therefore injecting sufferers with insulin is a good practice in treating the ailment. In type 2, administering insulin is as good as worsening the case, since the body already has excess and no longer observes it presence.

Early Treatment for Diabetes

Before the middle 19th century, there were no specific ways of combatting any of the two types of diabetes, type 1 was highly destructive until the discovery of insulin in 1921. On the other hand, type 2 was not rampant, because it was normally noticed after 50 years of age and food was not readily available as it is today.

Many dietary systems were developed to treat diabetes, including the Allen's starvation treatment. These were successful in their own way and were widely acclaimed, but the only issue was their inability to differentiate between types 1 and 2 diabetes in their treatment. The discovery of insulin in 1921 actually made things better and clearer.

Since then, a lot advances have taken place as well; in spite of these advances, diabetes has remained an ever-threatening disease, more than it used to be in the past. Studies show that more Americans had diabetes and pre-diabetes in 2016 compared to previous years.

Why Fasting Works for Type 2 Diabetes

It is already an established truth that Type 2 Diabetes results from insulin resistance. Fasting comes in as a practice to reduce insulin levels in the body. Type 2 is typically the presence of excessive glucose. To take away the excessive glucose, you can abstain from food. Within this period of abstinence from food, your blood sugar levels will come down and once your blood sugar levels become normal, you are now free from diabetes.

One precaution I always advise people to take is to always monitor their progress. You need to check your sugar level from time to time during fasting. I also advise them to suspend their blood sugar medications whenever their fasting, so as not to go below the normal and required sugar levels.

CHAPTER 7: FASTING FOR A YOUNGER, SMARTER YOU

KEY TAKEAWAYS

- Fasting promotes longevity.
- It has anti-aging capacity.
- It promotes the secretion of growth hormones.
- Fasting boosts brain power.
- Fasting enables us to remain focused.

SUMMARY

Apart from the popular functions of treating obesity and Type 2 diabetes, fasting is also effective in other areas, one of which is to help you stay young, fresh and improve brain capacity.

Boosting Brainpower

Absence of food causes the brain to become more active than usual, when the brain is deprived of calories, it does not become dull. It instead becomes quicker in learning and better in just about any process.

Abel James Fasting All-Stars

Initially, my major concern with fasting was in its ability to increase growth hormone and reduce inflammation, but when I really engaged myself in fasting, I also observed that mental focus also increased tremendously. Just like other mammals, humans are most likely to develop greater memory capacities, brain power when starvation sets in. The senses are very sharp at these times and are capable doing outstanding things.

During fasting, paying attention to every detail is also achieved. Studies have shown that fasting helps us to be attentive all the more and it has no singular side effect on cognitive ability.

Calories reduction also share one common characteristic, they help boost the memory while also increasing synaptic activity in the brain.

Fasting All-Stars Robb Wolf

Fasting within the range of three to five days can renew the human immune system. Report reveals that it terminates inflammation and causes the body to become sensitive to insulin. If there abnormal cells, fasting tends to facilitate their destruction and ultimate removal from the body - a process described as apoptosis. These are the things that cause aging, since fasting deals with them, one can equally say that fasting has an anti-aging capacity.

Autophagy is a form of total clean-up undergone by the body to keep cellular components at check, through autophagy, the body gets rid of diseased cell components and after this has happened, new ones are generated to replace them.

Amy Berger Fasting All-Stars

The best way to initiate autophagy in the body is through fasting, fasting cleanses the body of all unwanted debris and this accounts to an accelerated rate of autophagy, especially for sufferers of inflammation.

Fasting also facilitates the secretion of growth hormones, helping the body to renew at all times while staying young. Fasting may also help to reduce the development of cancerous cells through autophagy.

CHAPTER 8: FASTING FOR HEART HEALTH

KEY TAKEAWAYS

1. Presence of high cholesterol can cause heart diseases.

2. Lipoprotein determines the types of cholesterol.

3. There is low density and high-density lipoproteins (LDL and HDL).

4. When the liver can no longer store glycogen, it converts the glucose to triglycerides.

5. Triglyceride can also cause heart diseases.

SUMMARY

High cholesterol in the blood is causative factor in cardiovascular diseases and can be managed. This is why cholesterol is often seen as a poison among the people. However, cholesterol is not a poison. It helps in building cell walls and prepare some hormones. In measuring cholesterol level, we often differentiate into low-density lipoprotein (bad) and high-density lipoprotein (good). Cholesterol moves in the bloodstream alongside proteins called lipoproteins. It is the lipoprotein that determines whether it is LDL or HDL, the cholesterol remains the same.

There is another type of fat called triglycerides, once the liver is exhausted in holding glycogen, the excess is converted to triglyceride and they are moved out of the liver as Very Low-Density Lipoprotein (VLDL).

Heart diseases are also associated with high levels of triglyceride in the body, almost as dangerous as low density lipoprotein cholesterol. On its own, triglyceride increases risk of heart disease by 61%.

High Cholesterol Isn't a Dietary Problem

Although intake of too much fat may result in high blood cholesterol, it is not right to abstain from cholesterol-containing food, this does not lower the level of cholesterol. The liver has been found to generate about 80% of the cholesterol in the body, so feeding on low-cholesterol food has little or no influence.

Why Fasting Lowers Cholesterol

When carbohydrates reduce in our diets, the liver also reduces its production of triglycerides (because it is normally excess carbohydrate that is converted to triglyceride). This translates in the reduction in LDL levels, hence their precursors - VLDL, are no longer available. This is exactly what fasting does, it begins from the root by reducing amount of food (carbohydrate) taken in.

CHAPTER 9: WHAT YOU NEED TO KNOW ABOUT HUNGER

KEY TAKEAWAYS

- Hunger reduces during intermittent fasting.

- The hunger to eat normally begins from the mind.

- We can learn to associate some things with food and they in turn trigger our hunger for food when we see them.

- You need to get rid of the mind-set that regular eating is what you need to survive.

- While fasting, avoid sweeteners as much as possible.

SUMMARY

Hunger has always been one of the factors that discourage people from fasting, some are afraid that they would eat just too much after fasting or that they cannot just control hunger. Practically speaking, many of my patients have confessed that their hunger reduced drastically during intermittent fasting, instead of increasing uncontrollably. And like expected it is a surprise to most people who had expected the opposite.

Hunger Starts in the Mind

We often believe that hunger is a natural part of the human physiology, and that once we do not eat, it becomes inevitable. Hunger as it were, is not a sign of the quantity of food you've consumed, it reflects instead what we have associated with - it is not organic, it is learned. We learn to become hungry in occasions where food is displayed or when we perceive them. A telephone call to come for dinner can make us hungry even when we never felt it before then. Ivan Pavlov was able to show through his studies that dogs salivate when they see food, then they build their expectations around the sighted food. The dogs were usually fed by laboratory assistants, so the dogs learned to associate laboratory coat with feeding. In a little while, they began to salivate on seeing laboratory coats, even when no food is attached.

Hunger starts with the eye, we see things and become hungrier in response to their appearance. It can also be timed, if we habitually feed at a particular time, we are also likely to become hungry once that time approaches.

Defeating Hunger Conditioning

To go past conditioned hunger, we can undertake intermittent fasting as a tool. When we willingly skip meals and stay off food for some time, such appetites will be suppressed and ultimately be defeated.

In order to succeed at fasting, you will also need to get rid of the mind-set that you need to be eating at all time to stay strong and healthy. The best way to dissociate yourself from such is by eating only on your table, resist eating any other place like the car, computer desk, etc.

While fasting, avoid sweeteners as much as possible, if you must use, it must be in minute quantity. Strive to stay far from the cues that trigger food consumption during fast; it makes it a lot easier, do not depend on your will power.

Finally, hunger is not an excruciating experience as perceive it to be, it comes as fading wave instead. You have to know that these waves come and go in a little time, they do not last.

CHAPTER 10: WHO SHOULD NOT FAST?

KEY TAKEAWAYS

- People who do not have access to proper feeding should not fast.

- Children below 18 years should not consider fasting.

- Fasting is not advisable for pregnant and breastfeeding women.

- People with certain disease conditions like gastroesophageal reflux disease, should seek guidance before fasting.

- If you're already on medications, seek medical advice before fasting.

SUMMARY

The next important question we need to address is on who should and who should not fast. There are categories of people who need never consider fasting and their others who will need to be careful in their fasting programs to avoid certain mishaps.

The following groups of people are not supposed to ever fast:

- People who are not properly nourished or underweight.
- Children who are not yet up to 18 years of age.
- Pregnant women and breastfeeding women.

This does not imply that these ones can eat as they wish, or eat excessively.

The following will also need the guidance of a physician before they undertake fasting programs:

a. People with gout

b. Those taking drugs/medications.

c. Sufferers of Type 1 or Type 2 Diabetes.

d. Sufferers of gastroesophageal reflux disease.

Importantly, people with anorexia are already malnourished and underweight are not advised to go on therapeutic fasting. However, fasting does not cause anorexia, it is a psychological disorder and has nothing to do with not eating.

Should Women Fast?

The answer is a big Yes! Women can fast and can gain the same benefits from fasting as men do. Except in the cases mentioned above, women are free to fast on any range, and the results are same in both genders. The most important thing to learn is that you should consult your doctor once you start feeling inadequate or the results do not meet your expectations.

PART II: HOW TO FAST: CHAPTER 11: KINDS OF FASTS AND BEST PRACTICES

KEY TAKEAWAYS

- Fasts can be categorized according to their duration and according to what is allowed.
- In water-only fasts, all other fluids are prohibited.
- Juice fasts allow the consumption of all kinds of fluids.
- Fat fasts allow one to take pure fats while fasting.
- Juice fasts and fat fasts are not considered true fasts.

SUMMARY

For a very useful purpose, we classify fasts based on the duration and then what is acceptable within the fast. Here we concentrate on the later.

Mostly, fasts are done without any drink that contains calories, in other words, one can take drinks that are calories-free like black coffee, water and tea.

There is the water-only fast which is the usual kind obtainable in many societies, here other beverages are prohibited and it involves zero intake of salt. Recent modifications allow people to drink salt water within the fasting period since the body cannot retain water in the absence of salt. However, when the fasting time is moderated, salt deficiency should not be a problem.

There is also juice fasting which allows participants to drink water and juice within the fasting period. Juices naturally contain calories and sugars, so this is sometimes not considered a true fast.

Fat fasts is also a variety of fasting, but is not a true fast since one can consume pure fats like butter, coconut oil, etc. Many people like this fat fasting, saying that it makes fasting less difficult by reducing hunger. The argument remains that having little quantity of such fats will not alter the expected result of the fast.

When fasting is "dry", one is forbidden from taking any kind of fluid. Muslims normally practice this during the Ramadan period. Medically, I do not recommend this kind of fasting because of the accompanying dehydration. The risk of complication is also increased by dry fasts. All kinds of fasting can have healing effects if they are well structured and practiced.

CHAPTER 12: INTERMITTENT FASTING

KEY TAKEAWAYS

- Fasting regularly between meals is termed intermittent fasting.

- Short fasting lasts for less than 24 hours.

- Fasting duration depends on what suits the needs of an individual.

- Longer fasts last more than 24 hours.

- Long and extended fasts yield quicker results than the short ones.

SUMMARY

I have been able to show from previous chapters that fasting is not a harmful practice, and that it has many health benefits - combating obesity and type 2 diabetes.

Intermittent fasting simply refers to a structure where one fasts regularly, between the meal periods. The length and specifications of fasting varies a great deal from person to person and according to the need at hand.

Fasting is short when it is less than twenty-four hours, long when it is above 24 hours, though this can still be modified to suit other plans. Short fasts is the easiest and most practiced kind of fasting, people prefer it for its less demands and because it can fit into other daily activities like study, work, etc.

However, long or extended fasting periods give quicker results than the shorter ones, they are practiced less frequently anyway. Overall, all fasting schedules are not easy at fast, you only get used to it with consistent practice.

12-Hour Fasts

Until 1970s, 12-hour fast was only a normal practice, food cues were not scattered as it is today, so people normally ate three times between 7.am and 7.pm. This is followed by an involuntary fast from 7pm till 7am when they take breakfast - they 'break their fast'. The result of this practice was evident as obesity was not a problem to worry about.

16-Hour Fasts/Time-restricted Eating

Here, the schedule of daily meal is structured to have a sixteen-hour incorporated fast. For instance, people can fast fours in the morning (7-11am) then feed from then till 7pm, the remaining 12 hours makes it 16 hours of fast.

20-Hour Fasting: "The Warrior Diet"

The times at which meals are taken are as much important as the contents of the food itself, Ori Hoftmekler developed a feeding plan where all meals are taken in the evening within a four-hour window. This amounted to twenty hours of fast, he called this the warrior diet.

The entire idea is to time the eating plan, and structure it in such a way that various fasting practices can be incorporated for optimum health and treatment of already existing infirmities.

CHAPTER 13: LONGER PERIODS OF FASTING

KEY TAKEAWAYS

- Longer fasts can result in medical complications.

- Complications arise easily when the patient is under medication.

- Combining medication and fasting may make one glycemic.

- While fasting for longer periods, eat calories as usual.

- Once you notice any discomfort during fasting, quit and speak to your doctor.

SUMMARY

In the opening part we talked about how insulin resistance yields type 2 diabetes; short fasts can actually help in reversing the insulin levels but cannot maintain the kind of consistency required to tackle it completely, therefore, long fasts are required to put insulin levels low and keep them low as well.

The Risks and benefits of Longer Fasts

Like already pointed out, longer fasts are highly essential in treating type 2 diabetes and obesity, but there are also risks of complications associated with it. This is even more in diabetic patients and people who are under medications. I always advise my patients to speak up once they feel uncomfortable within the fast, fasting should make you feel hungry, and never make you sick. Ordinarily, you are supposed to consult your doctor before embarking on fasting programs or before adjusting your dietary plan, the doctor monitors these processes to avoid complications.

If you take the same medications as you would when you were not fasting, you are most likely to suffer glycaemia, this is often characterized by tremors, sweating and confusion. If this is not treated immediately, it progresses into seizures, loss of consciousness and death in extreme cases.

Twenty-four Hour Fast

In a 24-Hour fast, you fast from one meal to another, say from breakfast to breakfast or from dinner to dinner. You still get to take one meal daily and as much can take your medications (if any) without causing harm to yourself. It is usually preferred when you will have a busy day; you end up spending the entire day without food, and then take one meal in the evening. It saves cost and time, and because you still eat all, you need not worry about nutrient deficiency.

While engaging in longer fasts, it is not advisable to deliberately eat less calories.

There is another approach called the **5:2 Diet**, here you have your meals in normalcy for five days in a week, then you fast in the remaining two days. The two fast days can consecutive or spaced into different days, however it suits you most.

There is also **alternate-day fasting,** where fasting is done every other day. it is a little bit higher than the 5:2 plan since it is daily, it should be maintained until desired weight is achieved and then it can be reduced just to maintain the already attained weight.

In 36-Hour fast, the fast does not allow you to eat anything in a complete day, you eat today and skip the entire meals of the next day.

CHAPTER 14: EXTENDED FASTING

KEY TAKEAWAYS

- Extended fasts last longer than 42 hours.

- Insulin assists the retention of water and salt by the kidney

- During Extended fasts, the brain depends more on ketone to generate energy.

- While doing extended fasting, bowel movements slow down.

- Phosphorous depletion leads to refeeding syndrome.

SUMMARY

Extended fasts are fasts that last longer than 42 hours. Many Reports have shown that extended fasts are effective in treating obesity safely and other infirmities like diabetes.

Insulin promotes the retention of salt and water by the kidney, when we fast, the body excretes more water and salt because insulin level must have been reduced.

What to Expect During an Extended Fast

In fasting (extended fasting), it is usually very difficult at first, the hunger seems to be terrible at the initial stage, but as the days progress, it becomes easier and before you know it, it becomes a norm.

During Extended fast, there is reduction in the dependence of the brain on the use of glucose as source of energy. The burning fat generates ketone which the brain utilizes. Ketones are better fuels than glucose and as such can bring out improved mental capacity.

Extended fasting seldom results in abnormalities in electrolytes level - chloride urea, calcium, potassium, sodium and bicarbonate all retain their regular limits. Bowel movements may also slow down during extended fasting because nothing much gets to the digestive system.

The duration a fast can take all depends on the issues to be handled and the general preference of the patient. It could be 2-3 days, 7-14 days, or just above 42 hours.

Refeeding Syndrome

Refeeding Refers to the first one or two days that succeeds an extended fast. It does not happen to people with sufficient stores of fat, though it can occur when you fast for more than five days at a time. Refeeding syndrome typically happens when phosphorous-depletion occurs due to improper feeding. However, refeeding syndrome occurs more when people are starved, not regularly with fasting. To prevent this syndrome, you should not use the water-only plan for extended fasts, drink other fluids to enhance sustainability. Again, properly do all other activities like exercise programs during your fast, this helps to keep the bones and muscles in the way they should be.

CHAPTER 15: FASTING TIPS AND FAQS

KEY TAKEAWAYS

- Always bear your target in mind during fasting.

- Monitor your progress from time to time.

- Seek medical assistance when you no longer feel comfortable

- Try to drink enough water at the beginning of your fast each day.

- Being busy helps you to conquer hunger waves.

SUMMARY

Fasting is a normal activity that we sometimes do without knowing. There is no specific strategy that is unquestionably considered the best for fasting, but there are some essential tips that can make fasting successful. The first is that you should always bear your target in mind and never lose sight of it. You should also structure your fasting to produce the kind of result you need, watch your progress and know when to stop or when to change your plan for better results.

During fasting:

1. Try to drink water at the start of each day

2. Keep yourself very busy, it helps to curtail hunger for food.

3. Use mild suppressants like coffee

4. Learn to endure the waves of hunger as they come and go

5. Do not broadcast your fasting intentions.

6. Work with dietary plans when not fasting. etc.

Breaking Your Fast

Be gentle about breaking your fast, especially when it is a longer or extended fast. If you overeat at the close of your fast, you are likely to develop discomfort in the stomach. You can begin with a simple snack, then proceed to the main meal and eat just normal quantity, do not eat according to the instinct to eat much after fasting.

There are many concerns surrounding fasting, but these concerns are always the opposite. During fasting, you will not be overwhelmed by any of the following:

a. Hunger

b. Weakness/dizziness

c. Headaches

d. Constipation

e. Muscle Cramp

These things may arise at the initial phase of the fast, but they will all die down with time, experience and endurance.

Note also that:

Fasting will not make you cranky.

Fasting will not make you tired.

Fasting does not make one forgetful or confused.

You can exercise while fasting.

PART III: RESOURCES

Fasting Fluids

These are the fluids you can consume during fasting:

Water

Coffee

Tea and

Homemade broth.

24-Hour Fasting Protocol

In this fasting protocol, you can fast from dinner of one day to the dinner of the next day or from the lunch of one day to the lunch of the next day. This is going to be done three times per week. In other words, you have three fasting days in a week and four fasting-free days. On the fast-free days, I suggest you take on a diet that does not have much of refined carbohydrates and high in natural fats.

36-Hour Fasting Protocol

Here, you will fast for a complete day for three times in a week. The days can be consecutive or spaced from one another. This protocol is more effective in weight loss than the 24-hour regimen. On your eating days, eat more of natural fats and less of refined carbohydrates.

42-Hour Fasting Protocol

In this regimen, you will also fast for the whole day for three days every week. Additionally, will have to miss breakfast daily - weather or not you are fasting. Try to eat only whole food and stay off processed food.

7-to-14-Day Fasting Protocol

This protocol demands that you fast for about seven to fourteen days consecutively without any form of food or snack. You can only take fasting fluids like water, coffee, etc. It is a very intensive kind of fast and should never be underwent without the supervision of a medical doctor.

RECIPES

Recipes? Well, "yes", recipes!

And, of course, you are wondering what recipes are doing in a book on fasting! Well, here's why recipes are included in this book.

There are two parts to a comprehensive, healthy eating plan. The first part is *feeding* (that is the part where you actually eat something). The second part is *fasting* (the part where you do **not** eat anything). In this book, we have talked mostly about the second part (fasting), but not much about the first part (feeding). But the fact remains that a comprehensive, healthy eating plan must still pay attention to and ensure a healthy balance between the two parts (*feeding and fasting*). In short, it is crucial for you to ensure that you eat a heathy diet even as you also fast, intermittently. The recipes below meet the requirements of part one of a comprehensive, healthy eating plan (*feeding*). They are good additions to a healthy eating pattern and you can incorporate them into a 24-hour fasting protocol or into a 42-hour fasting protocol. So, check out these recipes. They are delicious and fun!

Kevlar Coffee

NOTE: You may consume Kevlar coffee once a day, on fast days, between your wake-up time and your normal lunch time (if you are not doing lunch). It will help you feel full and satisfied. This recipe is for 1 cup. The preparation time for this recipe is about 3 minutes.

INGREDIENTS: 1 cup of brewed coffee, 1 or 2 tablespoons of heavy whipping cream (no less than 35% fat), 1 or 2 tablespoons of butter, and 1 or 2 tablespoons of MCT oil or coconut oil.

DIRECTIONS: (1) Measure equal parts of cream, coconut oil and butter and add to the coffee. (2) Using an immersion blender, blend until it becomes creamy. (3) Enjoy!

Crushed Nuts 'n' Berry Parfait

NOTE: This recipe is for 2 servings. The preparation time for this recipe is 20 to 35 minutes.

INGREDIENTS: You will need the following ingredients: Half cup of heavy whipping cream (no less than 35% fat), 12 blueberries, 8 crushed walnuts, 8 crushed almonds, 4 diced strawberries, One-third cup of blackberries, One-third cup of raspberries.

OPTIONAL INGREDIENTS: You may need the following optional ingredients: 1 tablespoon of pure cocoa powder (100%), 1 teaspoon of pure vanilla extract, half tablespoon of ground flaxseed, half tablespoon of chia seeds, 1 tablespoon of cinnamon, for serving.

DIRECTIONS: (1) Put whipping cream in bowl. Add the vanilla extract (optional and cocoa powder (optional) and stir. (2) Whip the cream with a hand mixer for about 2 to 4 minutes. (3) Add the berries and nuts into the whipped cream and stir. (4) *Optional:* If you are using the ground chia seeds and flaxseed, you may mix them in. Also, if you are using the cinnamon, you may sprinkle it over the top. (5) Optional: For a nice chilly and cooling effect on a hot summer day, leave the bowl of whipped cream in the freezer for about 30 to 40 minutes. (6) Enjoy!

Gulasciutto Salad

NOTE: This is a great tasting salad with arugula and prosciutto as the signature ingredients. This recipe is for 1 serving. The preparation time is about 15 minutes.

INGREDIENTS:
8 to 10 thin slices of prosciutto, 2 to 4 cups of washed arugula, half cup of olives, sliced, and half cup tomato, chopped. For the dressing you will need: 1 teaspoon of balsamic vinegar and 1 tablespoon of extra-virgin olive oil.

DIRECTIONS: (1) Place the prosciutto, arugula, olives and tomato in a bowl and toss together. (2) For the dressing, mix the vinegar and olive oil together, properly. (3) Toss the salad and dressing together. Optionally, the dressing may be served on the side. (4) Enjoy!

Perugula Pine Nuts Salad

NOTE: This is a great tasting salad with arugula, pear and pine nuts as the signature ingredients. This recipe is for 2 servings. The preparation time is about 15 minutes.

INGREDIENTS: 1 thinly sliced pear, 3 to 5 cups of washed arugula, ½ cup of pine nuts, 5 tablespoons of extra-virgin olive oil, Some ground black pepper and Himalayan salt, and ½ lemon.

DIRECTIONS: (1) Place the arugula, pine nuts and pear slices in a bowl and toss together. (2) For the dressing, squeeze some juice from the half lemon over the salad. And pour some olive oil on top of the salad. (3) Season the salad with the pepper and salt. (4) Enjoy!

Cauliflower "No Grains" Pizza

NOTE: No grain flour for this pizza! Just a healthy and great tasting cauliflower alternative - the cauliflower "no grains" pizza! Its scrumptious and healthy! This recipe will give you 1 pizza of about 8 inches which is equal to 3 servings. The preparation time is about 15 minutes and the cooking time is about 30 to 40 minutes.

INGREDIENTS: 1 ½ cups of cauliflower florets, 1 teaspoon of powdered garlic, 1 teaspoon of Himalayan salt, 1 teaspoon of dried oregano, 2 lightly beaten eggs, and any healthy choice of pizza toppings.

DIRECTIONS: (1) Oven should be preheated to 400 degrees Fahrenheit and a baking sheet should be lined with parchment paper. (2) Using a food processor, pulse the cauliflower florets until they are finely chopped, then place in a bowl. (3) Add the eggs, oregano, garlic powder and Himalayan salt into the bowl of finely chopped cauliflower and mix well. (4) Place the cauliflower mixture in the center of the baking sheet that you had lined with parchment paper and using your hands, knead the mixture to form a pizza crust. (5) Bake until lightly golden which should be for about 20 minutes. (6) Add your choice of healthy toppings. (7) Bake for additional 10 to 20 minutes. (8) Enjoy!

Bacon Wrapped Chicken Drumsticks

NOTE: Here's a tasty chicken drumstick recipe for ya! This recipe is for 2 servings. The preparation time is about 8 minutes and cooking time is between 40 and 50 minutes.

INGREDIENTS: 4 chicken drumsticks, 4 bacon slices, 1 teaspoon of ground black pepper, and 1 ½ teaspoons of Himalayan salt.

DIRECTIONS: (1) Oven should be preheated to 400 degrees Fahrenheit and a baking sheet should be lined with aluminum foil. (2) Wrap one slice of bacon around one drumstick, starting from the bottom to the top of the drumstick to the top. (3) Place the drumsticks on the baking sheet that you had lined with aluminum foil. (4) Season the drumsticks with the pepper and salt. (5) Bake until the bacon looks crispy which should be for about 40 to 50 minutes. (6) Enjoy!

Roasted CauliRice

NOTE: The roasted caulirice is a healthy great-tasting roasted cauliflower meal that looks like rice. The preparation time is 10 minutes and the cooking time is about 15 to 20 minutes.

INGREDIENTS: 1 head of cauliflower, ½ tablespoon of Himalayan salt.

DIRECTIONS:

(1) Oven should be preheated to 400 degrees Fahrenheit and a baking sheet should be lined with parchment paper. (2) Cut the cauliflower into florets. Remove the stems. (3) Pulse the cauliflower florets in a food processor until it resembles rice or grate the cauliflower by hand. (4) Spread the cauliflower rice on the baking sheet that you had lined with parchment paper. (5) Sprinkle with salt. (6) Bake for about 10 to 15 minutes. Flip the cauliflower rice every 5 minutes and do not allow the cauliflower rice to brown. (7) Add your choice of spices or herbs. (8) Enjoy!

StrawKale Berry Salad

NOTE: This is a nice salad with strawberry and kale as the signature ingredients. This recipe is for 2 servings. The preparation time is about 15 minutes.

INGREDIENTS: 4 or 5 cups of kale, 12 to 16 diced strawberries, diced, 1 cup of walnuts, 5 tablespoons of extra-virgin olive oil, I tablespoon of balsamic vinegar, and some ground black pepper and Himalayan salt.

DIRECTIONS: (1) Place the strawberries, kale and walnuts in a bowl and toss together. (2) For the dressing, pour the olive oil and the balsamic vinegar on top of the salad. (3) Season the salad with the pepper and salt. (4) Enjoy!

NOTES

NOTES

NOTES

NOTES

RECOMMENDED FOR YOU!

- SUMMARY OF CLEAN & LEAN BY IAN K. SMITH M.D. — 30 Days, 30 Foods, a New You! — BY Dependable Publishing
- SUMMARY OF THE LONGEVITY PARADOX BY DR. STEVEN R. GUNDRY, MD — How to Die Young at a Ripe Old Age — BY Dependable Publishing
- SUMMARY OF BEST SELF BOOK BY MIKE BAYER — BE YOU, ONLY BETTER — BY Dependable Publishing
- SUMMARY OF ATOMIC HABITS BOOK BY JAMES CLEAR — An Easy & Proven Way to Build Good Habits & Break Bad Ones — BY Dependable Publishing
- SUMMARY OF 12 RULES FOR LIFE BY JORDAN B. PETERSON — An Antidote to Chaos — BY Dependable Publishing
- SUMMARY OF BRIEF ANSWERS TO THE BIG QUESTIONS BOOK BY STEPHEN HAWKING — BY DEPENDABLE PUBLISHING
- SUMMARY OF CAN'T HURT ME BY DAVID GOGGINS — MASTER YOUR MIND AND DEFY THE ODDS — BY DEPENDABLE PUBLISHING
- SUMMARY OF MAYBE YOU SHOULD TALK TO SOMEONE BOOK BY LORI GOTTLIEB — A Therapist, HER Therapist, and Our Lives Revealed — BY DEPENDABLE PUBLISHING
- SUMMARY OF DR. COLBERT'S HORMONE HEALTH ZONE BOOK BY DON COLBERT — Lose Weight, Restore Energy, Feel 25 Again! — BY DEPENDABLE PUBLISHING

SUMMARY OF STRESS LESS ACCOMPLISH MORE
BOOK BY EMILY FLETCHER
Meditation For Extraordinary Performance
BY
DEPENDABLE PUBLISHING

SUMMARY OF UNDER PRESSURE
BY LISA DAMOUR
CONFRONTING THE EPIDEMIC OF STRESS AND ANXIETY IN GIRLS
BY
DEPENDABLE PUBLISHING

SUMMARY OF THE LIFE-CHANGING MAGIC OF TIDYING UP
BY MARIE KONDO
The Japanese Art of Decluttering and Organizing
BY
DEPENDABLE PUBLISHING

SUMMARY OF MOSTLY SUNNY
BY JANICE DEAN
How I Learned to Keep Smiling Through the Rainiest Days
BY
DEPENDABLE PUBLISHING

SUMMARY OF IT'S NOT SUPPOSED TO BE THIS WAY
BOOK BY LYSA TERKEURST
Finding Unexpected Strength When Disappointments Leave You Shattered
BY
DEPENDABLE PUBLISHING

SUMMARY OF DARE TO LEAD
BOOK BY BRENE BROWN
Brave Work. Tough Conversations. Whole Hearts.
BY
DEPENDABLE PUBLISHING

SUMMARY OF THE GREENPRINT
BOOK BY MARCO BORGES
Plant-Based Diet, Best Body, Better World
BY
DEPENDABLE PUBLISHING

SUMMARY OF THE THEFT OF AMERICA'S SOUL
BY PHIL ROBERTSON
Blowing the Lid Off the Lies That Are Destroying Our Country
BY
Dependable Publishing

SUMMARY OF NEXT LEVEL BASIC
BOOK BY STASSI SCHROEDER
The Definitive Basic Bitch Handbook
BY
DEPENDABLE PUBLISHING